Task Listening

Task Listening

Student's Book

Lesley Blundell and Jackie Stokes

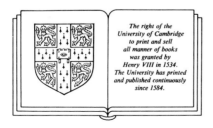

The right of the
University of Cambridge
to print and sell
all manner of books
was granted by
Henry VIII in 1534.
The University has printed
and published continuously
since 1584.

Cambridge University Press
Cambridge
London   New York   New Rochelle
Melbourne   Sydney

Published by the Press Syndicate of the University of Cambridge
The Pitt Building, Trumpington Street, Cambridge CB2 1RP
32 East 57th Street, New York, NY 10022, USA
10 Stamford Road, Oakleigh, Melbourne 3166, Australia

© Cambridge University Press 1981

First published 1981
Fifth printing (with corrections) 1983
Ninth printing 1987

Printed in Great Britain
at the University Press, Cambridge

ISBN 0 521 23135 3 Student's Book
ISBN 0 521 23136 1 Teacher's Book
ISBN 0 521 23137 X Cassette

LC

Contents

Acknowledgements

The authors would like to thank Mrs H. A. Swan and the staff of the Swan School, Oxford, for testing this material. They would also like to thank the following for taking part in the recording: Judith Bennett, Jon Blundell, Mrs P. Brown, Marilena di Gennaro, Margaret Flynn, Elizabeth Fox, Stuart Haggar, Michael Martin, Fiona Morison, Ray Murphy, Helen Naylor, Michael Parsley, Felicity Preedy, Peter Ratcliffe, Christopher Richards, Yumiko Seshimo, Rodney Smith, H. A. Swan, Ruth Swan, Thomas Swan and Stephen Woolgar.

Illustrations and extracts are reproduced by kind permission of the following: British Railways Board (pp. 2 and 3); British Airways (p. 5); Associated Book Publishers Ltd: cartoons from *Penelope* (p. 7) and *Angels on Horseback and Elsewhere* by Norman Thelwell (p. 49); Andre Deutsch Ltd: extract from *How to be an Alien* by George Mikes (p. 7); Consumers' Association: cartoon from *Handyman Which?* (p. 7) and extract from *Which? Car Buying Guide 1975* (p. 37); Punch Publications Ltd: cartoon by Raymonde (p. 7); Wales Tourist Board (p. 9); Midland Bank Ltd (pp. 14 and 15); Duckworth and Co. Ltd: illustration from *Inventions* by W. Heath Robinson (p. 19); Automobile Association (p. 21); Drive Publications Ltd: material from *AA Book of the Car* (p.25); Adkin and Co. (pp. 26 and 27); Royal Shakespeare Company (p. 43); J. Sainsbury Ltd (p. 45); J. Allan Cash Ltd (p. 46a, b, e and f); Private Eye Productions Ltd: cartoon by Ffolkes (p. 49); Syndication International Ltd (p. 50); William Collins Sons and Co. Ltd: quizzes from *The Armada Christmas Fun Book* compiled by Mary Danby (p. 51); Dateline International (p. 53).

Photographs by Maggie Stocking: pp. 23, 46c and d; by Stephen Woolgar: p. 52
Illustrations by Annie McManus: 4, 10, 16, 30, 31, 44, 48; by Chris Evans: pp. 6, 8, 15, 18, 32, 34
Cover illustration by Edward McLachan
Book design by Peter Ducker

Introduction

Task Listening helps make listening to English easy!

You may find it difficult to understand English spoken at normal speed because it seems too fast, and the language you have already learnt may seem incomprehensible when used in everyday conversation. These difficulties arise because you are probably trying to catch every word and are missing the overall message as a result. *Task Listening* will help you to listen for the *gist* of what someone is saying and to sift out the information you really need to know.

Task Listening consists of twenty-six units. In each unit you will hear a short tape recording and do some kind of practical exercise or task in your book, such as labelling a picture or filling in a grid. The recordings are of people speaking at normal speed in everyday situations. Each unit has as its theme a setting or situation in which listening plays a major part, for example at an airport listening for flight announcements or at a travel agency being told about different means of transport.

When you listen to the recording, remember, you don't need to understand every single word to get the general idea of what is being said and to do the task. For example, in unit 7 'Using a bank account' (page 14) there is a blank cheque. The setting for the recording is at the bank where a cashier is helping a foreign student to fill in a cheque. The task for you is to do just that. You may listen to the tape as many times as you want in order to glean all the relevant details to complete the task.

Besides the listening task, there are also reading and writing tasks related to the theme of the unit. So, for example, after filling in the cheque in unit 7 you have a look at a bank statement and fill in a banker's order.

1 Catching the right train

Listening

Fill in the details of the trains on the grid.

Destination	Platform Number	Time	Other Information
SOUTHAMPTON			
COVENTRY			
PLYMOUTH			
PADDINGTON			
CARDIFF			
YORK			

Reading and writing

32 Abercrombie Ave,
Coventry,
Sunday evening.

Dear Peter,

Thank you for your postcard from Italy. We were pleased to hear you enjoyed yourself.

Yes we'd love you to come on the 27th for the weekend. Why don't you get a train from Paddington after work on Friday? Write to us and say when you'll arrive at Coventry and we'll meet you at the station.

See you on Friday
Love from
Andrew and Jenny

Choose a suitable train for Peter to catch and complete his postcard to Andrew and Jenny.

London → Reading → Oxford → Banbury → Birmingham

Mondays to Saturdays

Stations: Paddington, Reading, Reading General, Didcot, Oxford, Banbury, Leamington Spa, Stratford-upon-Avon, Dorridge, Solihull, Coventry, Birmingham International, Birmingham New Street

— departures —   — arrivals —

Paddington	Reading	Didcot	Oxford	Banbury	Leamington Spa	Stratford-upon-Avon	Dorridge	Solihull	Coventry	Birmingham International	Birmingham New Street
			16 30	16 51	17 18	17 37	18 16	18 32	17 58	→	18 18
				17 15	17 42	18 02			18 21	→	18 40
15 50	16 20			17 36	→		→	→		18 28	18 41	18 58
	16 41	17 03	17 45	18 17							
16 25	17 04	17 03	18 36	18 58		19 27	20 16	19 42	19 48	20 28	20 41	20 06
16 25	17 04	18 20		19 07		20 14		21 02	21 08	21 04	21 27	20 58
17 30	18 00		19 29		20 31	20 50	21 31	21 56	22 02			21 40
17 42		18 46	19 48	20 05	20 50		23 17		22 58	→		23 21
18 06	18 57	19 30		20 20	22 21	22 41						
19 00	19 30		21 55								
20 50	21 20	21 38									

Dear Andrew & Jenny,

Thank you _____

I'm going to get the _____

_____ from Paddington. So

I will arrive at _____

I hope you'll be able to meet me.

See _____

_____

Be properly addressed
POSTCODE

Andrew & Jenny Brown
32 Abercrombie Ave.
Coventry

PLX14128

INTERNATIONAL
7 OCT 1980
C

Listening

Fill in the missing information.

Reading and writing

Mr Browning must be at his hotel in Frankfurt at 3.00 p.m. (15.00) for a meeting. It takes 30 minutes to get to his hotel from Frankfurt Airport. Complete the notes at the bottom of the page for him.

LONDON—FRANKFURT — British airways / Associated Hotels

DEPART London, Heathrow Airport. BA flights: Terminal 1 (Minimum check-in time at pier gate 20 mins) Other flights: Terminal 2 (Minimum check-in time 30 mins)
London, Gatwick Airport [G] (Minimum check-in time 30 mins)
ARRIVE Frankfurt-on-Main Airport

Frequency	Aircraft Dep	Arr	Via	Flight	Aircraft	Class & Catering	
Daily	0820	1045(y)	non-stop	BA724	TRD	FY	✗
Daily	1005	1230	non-stop	LH033	AB3	FY	✗
Daily	1105	1230	non-stop	LH033	AB3	FY	✗
Daily	1125	1350(y)	non-stop	BA726	TRD	FY	✗
Daily	1410	1635	non-stop	LH035	727	FY	✗
Daily	1455	1625	non-stop	LH035	727	FY	✗
Daily	1605[G]	1825(y)	non-stop	BA784	B11	Y	✗✗
Daily	1645	1910(y)	non-stop	BA728	L10 (a)	FY	✗
Daily	1750	1915	non-stop	BA730	TRD	FY	✗
Daily	1810	2035	non-stop	LH037	AB3	FY	✗
Daily	1850	2115	non-stop	BA730	TRD	FY	✗
Daily	1910	2035	non-stop	LH037	AB3	FY	✗

Class of service
F First class
Y Economy

Catering
✗ Meal — i.e. full breakfast, lunch, dinner or supper
✗✗ Flight snack/Continental breakfast/Refreshment/Afternoon tea

AIRPORT INFORMATION

Place	Transport to Airport Address and coach departure time (in minutes) before aircraft departure and other Surface Connections	Single Fare	Airport Minimum check-in time in mins.
BRITISH ISLES (cont.)			
London (LON)	Coaches depart Victoria Terminal at frequent intervals throughout the day for Terminals 1 and 3. Passengers for Terminal 2 alight at Terminals 1 and walk across connecting bridge. Telephone 01 821 4074/4075 for coach services. Passengers are advised to join a coach not later than: Terminal 1 (International flights)— 120 minutes before scheduled departure time of aircraft (165 minutes for flights to Tel Aviv). Terminal 1 (Inter-Britain flights)— 110 minutes before scheduled departure time of aircraft. Terminal 3 Coaches from Victoria Terminal: Minimum check-in time 2 hours 15 minutes before aircraft departure time. Terminal 2 Check-in times vary according to carrier and should be verified prior to departure.	£1.70 £1.70	See relevant schedule table
London (Gatwick)	Gatwick Airport. Frequent trains from Victoria Station	£3.15 (1st) £2.10 (2nd)	BA, EI, GT, SK 30Int.

FLIGHT ARRIVAL/DEPARTURE ENQUIRIES AT PRINCIPAL UK AIRPORTS

To obtain information concerning flight arrivals and departures, on the day of travel, at the following airports, telephone:—

Aberdeen	72-2331	Edinburgh	031-333 1000	London (Heathrow)	01-759 2525
Belfast	29271	Glasgow	041-887 1111	,, (Gatwick)	Crawley (0293) 502064
Birmingham	021-743 4272	Prestwick	0292 79822	Manchester	061-437 5277
Inverness	Ardersier 2280	Newcastle	Newcastle 869081		

Depart from .... Airport at ..... a.m.

Get to Airport from ....

Transport costs £.......

Leave ..... minutes before departure time of aircraft.

Be at Transport Terminal by ..... a.m.

Flight number ....   Type of aircraft ....

Food during flight ....   Arrival time ...... p.m.

If the weather is bad on day of flight, ring ....

for flight details.

Listening

Choose one of the places on the map and listen for the weather forecast for that area. Draw the correct symbol on the map.

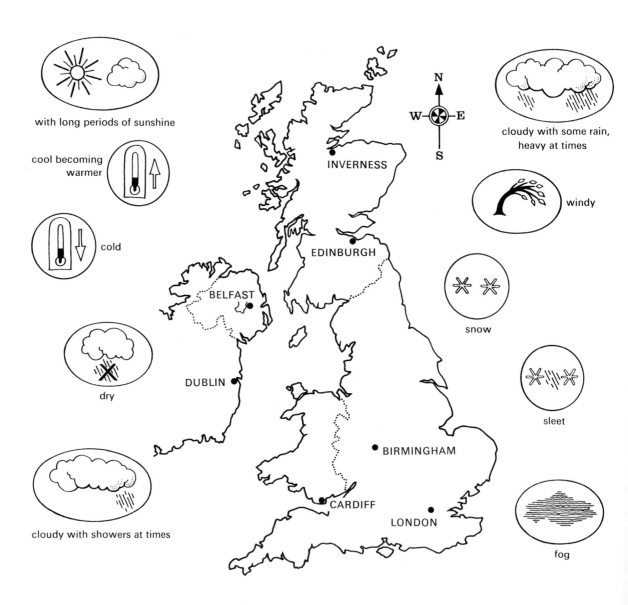

with long periods of sunshine

cool becoming warmer

cold

dry

cloudy with showers at times

cloudy with some rain, heavy at times

windy

snow

sleet

fog

INVERNESS

EDINBURGH

BELFAST

DUBLIN

BIRMINGHAM

CARDIFF

LONDON

Reading and writing

THE WEATHER

THIS is the most important topic in the land. Do not be misled by memories of your youth when, on the Continent, wanting to describe someone as exceptionally dull, you remarked: 'He is the type who would discuss the weather with you.' In England this is an ever-interesting, even thrilling topic, and you must be good at discussing the weather.

EXAMPLES FOR CONVERSATION
For Good Weather

'Lovely day, isn't it?'
'Isn't it *beautiful*?'
'The sun . . .'
'Isn't it gorgeous?'
'Wonderful, isn't it?'
'It's so nice and hot . . .'
'Personally, I think it's so nice when it's hot– isn't it?'
'I adore it – don't you?'

For Bad Weather

'Nasty day, isn't it?'
'Isn't it dreadful?'
'The rain . . . I hate rain . . .'
'I don't like it at all. Do you?'
'Fancy such a day in July. Rain in the morning, then a bit of sunshine, and then rain, rain, rain, all day long.'
'I remember exactly the same July day in 1936.'
'Yes, I remember too.'
'Or was it in 1928?'
'Yes, it was.'
'Or in 1939?'
'Yes, that's right.'

What do you think is being said in these cartoons? Write captions for each one.

4 Sightseeing

Listening

Put the correct number in the box beside each description. Then fill in the missing information.

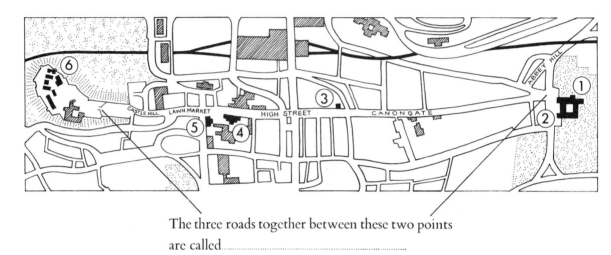

The three roads together between these two points
are called..

THINGS TO SEE IN EDINBURGH

☐ <u>Abbey</u>: built in .... by
King David of Scotland.

☐ <u>Heart of Midlothian</u> is a
heart-shaped design
in the ....

☐ <u>Edinburgh Castle</u>: part of
this, Queen Margaret's chapel
is the .... building
in Edinburgh.

☐ <u>John Knox House</u>: now a

....

☐ <u>The Palace of Holyrood</u> ....

☐ <u>St Giles's Cathedral</u>: where

.... preached.

Reading and writing

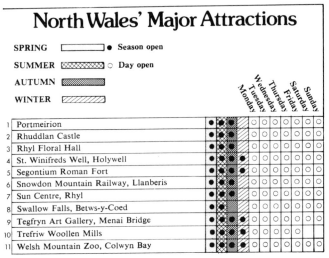

North Wales' Major Attractions

		SPRING ▭ ● Season open								
		SUMMER ▨ ○ Day open								
		AUTUMN ▨								
		WINTER ▨								

		Monday	Tuesday	Wednesday	Thursday	Friday	Saturday	Sunday		
1	Portmeirion	●	●	●		○	○	○	○	○
2	Rhuddlan Castle	●	●	●		○	○	○	○	○
3	Rhyl Floral Hall	●	●	●		○	○	○	○	○
4	St. Winifreds Well, Holywell	●	●	●	●	○	○	○	○	○
5	Segontium Roman Fort	●	●	●		○	○	○	○	○
6	Snowdon Mountain Railway, Llanberis	●	●	●		○	○	○	○	○
7	Sun Centre, Rhyl	●	●	●		○	○	○	○	○
8	Swallow Falls, Betws-y-Coed	●	●	●		○	○	○	○	○
9	Tegfryn Art Gallery, Menai Bridge	●	●	●	●	○	○	○	○	○
10	Trefriw Woollen Mills	●	●	●		○	○	○	○	
11	Welsh Mountain Zoo, Colwyn Bay	●	●	●	●	○	○	○	○	○

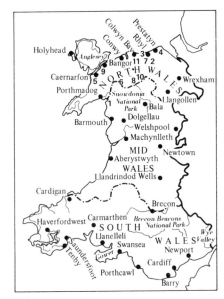

Write a postcard to an English friend about your holiday in Wales.

Rhuddlan's mighty castle.

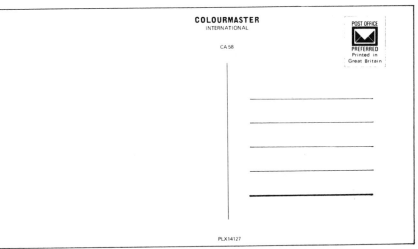

COLOURMASTER
INTERNATIONAL

CA 58

POST OFFICE
PREFERRED
Printed in
Great Britain

PLX14127

Hotels, Motels, Inns and Guest Houses

Town (County) Hotel Address Telephone number	Overnight bed and breakfast Min. £	Overnight bed and breakfast Max. £	Dinner, bed and breakfast Min. £	Weekly terms Dinner, bed and breakfast Min. £	Weekly terms Dinner, bed and breakfast Max. £	Full board Min. £	Full board Max. £	Number of letting rooms	Private	Public	Period open months 1-12	Other facilities
TREFRIW												
Gwynedd (Caernarvonshire)												
Inn												
Ye Olde Ship T. Llanrwst 640013			7·50					3		1	1-12	P ✕ C ▣
Guest Houses												
Argoed T. Llanrwst 640091				32·00				2	1	1		P UL ✂ C
Gaynor House T. Llanrwst 640208	3·50		7·00	35·00				2 2 3	1	1	1-12	P UL ✕ C ▣
Trefriw Wells T. Llanrwst 640057	5·50		10·00					1 4	1	1	1-12	P ✕ C ▣
Private Houses												
Belmont, Ffordd Crafnant												
T. Llanrwst 640463			7·00	35·00				2		1	4-10	P UL ✕ C ▣
Kendal T. Llanrwst 640200		3·25		35·00				2 1		1	1-12	P UL C ▣
Tan-y-Coed T. Llanrwst 640766	3·50	4·00	6·00	35·00				4 1		1	1-12	P UL ✕ C ▣

P Outdoor parking available.

UL Not licensed for sale of alcoholic drinks.

✕ Dogs not allowed under any circumstances. If this symbol does not appear it is still adviseable to contact the establishment concerned.

✂ Childrens cots and high chairs and baby sitting/listening service available.

C Reduced Rates for children.

▣ Ironing facilities available for guests use.

5 Finding out the house rules

Listening

Put a cross on the picture where the rule is being broken. Make brief notes of each rule.

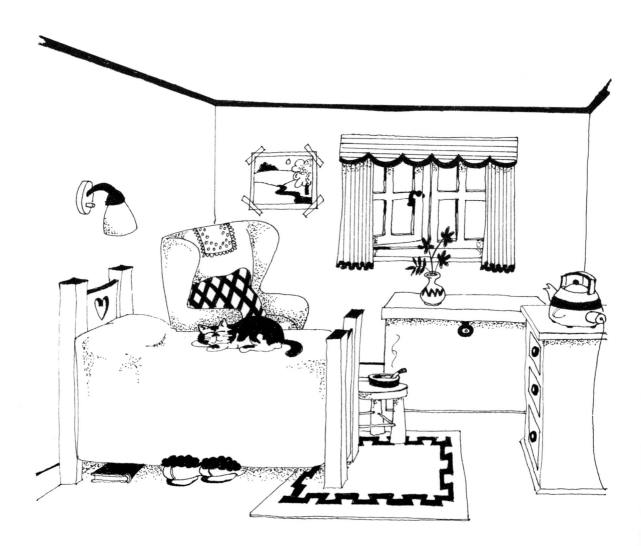

Reading and writing

You are staying at a hotel. Read the notices below.

On arrival   Find your room. Put a circle round the number on the plan.
Find the fire exit. Put 'FE' on the plan and draw a line from your room to the exit.
Find the nearest fire extinguisher. Put a circle round the symbol on the plan.

On departure   Pay bill for 7 nights = £..

Where do I leave the key?..

Can I leave my room after lunch?..

Can I pay by cheque?..

It is essential that all guests read this notice.

Fire Precautions

If you detect a fire
1.   Sound the fire alarm.
2.   For small local outbreaks, and if there is no personal danger, try to put out the fire by using the nearest extinguisher.

In the event of fire
1.   Warning bells/sirens will ring continuously.
2.   Close all doors and windows.
3.   Evacuate the Hotel by using: —
your nearest exit, which is

TURN LEFT THEN RIGHT
. . . .
TO EXIT
. . . .

General Information

Vacating Rooms
Bedrooms must be vacated by NOON on the day of departure. PLEASE LEAVE YOUR KEY WITH RECEPTION.

Cheques
We regret that cheques cannot be accepted unless supported by a bankers card.

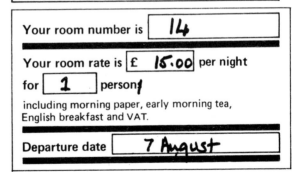

Your room number is   **14**

Your room rate is £ **15.00** per night

for   **1**   person

including morning paper, early morning tea, English breakfast and VAT.

Departure date   **7 August**

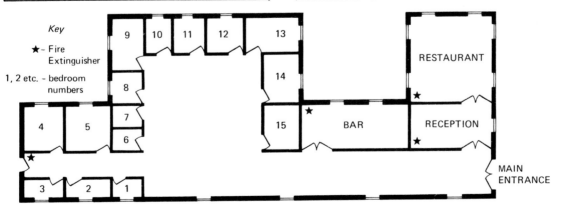

Key

★ – Fire Extinguisher

1, 2 etc. – bedroom numbers

9 10 11 12 13

RESTAURANT

14

8

7

15   BAR   RECEPTION

6

4   5

3   2   1

MAIN ENTRANCE

6 Phoning a flat-owner

Listening

Put a tick or a cross in the boxes.
Fill in the missing information.

Ring Oxford 40414 about
furnished flat
Find out: [✓] or [✗]
    Near City Centre   [ ]
    Near Shops   [ ]
    Garden   [ ]
    Central heating   [ ]
Visit tomorrow 5 p.m.   [ ]
Rent per month . . . . . .
Number of rooms . . . . . .
Floor . . . . . .
Name of landlord/landlady

    . . . .
Address . . . .

. . . .

Reading and writing

Using the other letters and the information on the tape to help you, write to the landlady to say that you would like to rent her flat.

_____ ,
_____)
_____ .

_____

Dear _____ ,
Following our _____
I would like to confirm
that I am interested in
renting your _____ for
_____ from _____
to _____ 19__ at _____
per _____ .

_____)
_____

21 York Street
Lambton
Yorks

3 February 1981

Conversation,
your flat
June 1982
per month.

Dear Mr Black,
Following
for one year
from June
at f

Yours Sincerely
Jeremy Thom

Listening

Fill in the blank cheque according to the instructions given by the bank cashier.

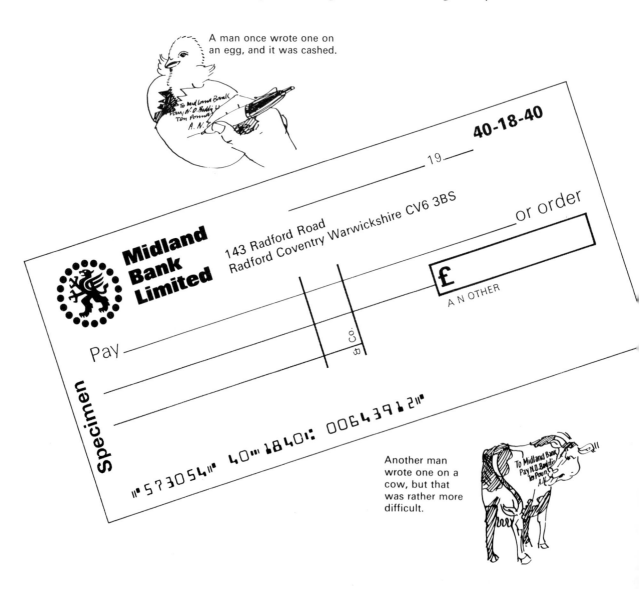

A man once wrote one on an egg, and it was cashed.

Another man wrote one on a cow, but that was rather more difficult.

Reading and writing

Which television can Mr A. N. Other afford to buy?
He wants to make the hire purchase payments by standing order. Fill in the form
for him. The TV shop, Jackson's Ltd, also banks with the Midland Bank in
Coventry. Their account number is 00456823.

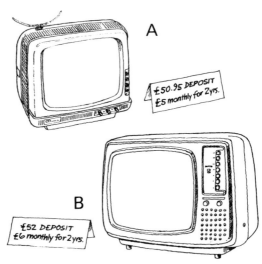

A

£50.95 DEPOSIT
£5 monthly for 2yrs.

B

£52 DEPOSIT
£6 monthly for 2yrs.

£57 DEPOSIT
£7 monthly for 2yrs.

C

Standing Order Mandate

TO _____ Bank Limited   Date _____

Address _____

	Bank	Branch Title *not address*	Sorting Code number
Please pay			
	Beneficiary		Account number
for the credit of			
	Amount in figures	Amount in words	
†the sum of	£		
	Date and amount of first payment		Date and frequency
commencing	*Now* * _____	£	and thereafter every
	Date and amount of last payment		
until		£	*until you receive further notice from me/us in writing
quoting the reference			and debit my/our account accordingly.

*This instruction cancels any previous order in favour of the beneficiary named above, under this reference.
*Delete as appropriate
†If the amounts of periodic payments vary they should be incorporated in a schedule overleaf.

Special instructions

Signature/s _____   _____

Title of account and
account number to be debited _____

Note: The Bank will not undertake to
a) make any reference to Value Added Tax or pay a stated sum plus V.A.T.
b) advise remitter's address to beneficiary.
c) advise beneficiary of inability to pay.
d) request beneficiary's banker to advise beneficiary of receipt.

Standing orders and direct
debiting are just two of
the services available
when you have a current
account.
With a standing order you
tell us about regular bills
of a fixed amount like
rent, rates and H.P.
payment, and we
remember to pay them
out of your money. You
just sign a form like the
one shown here.

8 Leaving a message

Listening

Which picture best represents the message?
Put a tick beside the correct one.

Reading and writing

Where would you expect to see these notices?

WANTED

GOOD HOMES for
Labrador Puppies
7 weeks old.
Tel : 96701

FOR SALE
Slazenger tennis
racquet, hardly
used. £8 o.n.o.
Tel 55944

3 PINTS
TODAY
PLEASE

LONDON

COACH FOR LONDON
LEAVES SCHOOL AT 8 A.M.
SATURDAY
DON'T BE LATE.

CAR
PARK
FULL

CLOSED
FOR LUNCH 1–2.15

You have to go out for half an hour.
Write a message to leave on your door for a friend
who is arriving today.

JOHN
Gone to work!
Milk, butter in fridge.
Cornflakes, bread, jam in
cupboard. Help yourself!
See you later.
Peter.

17

Listening

Label the three dials and use arrows to show their settings for washing white sheets and towels. Mark where the powder is put and note how much to use.

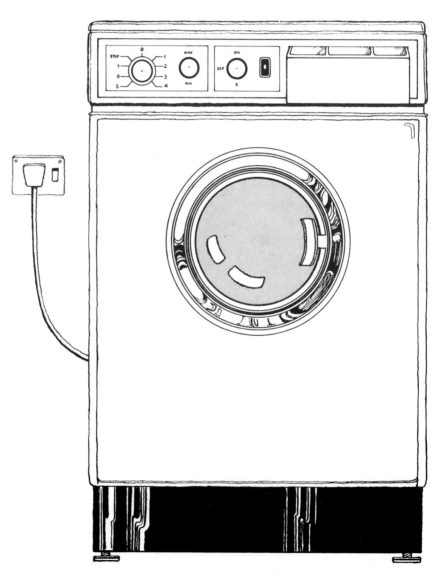

Reading and writing

The Anti-Litter Machine

The mechanism is simple.
A barrel of gum drips slowly onto a large wooden wheel and a brush evenly distributes the sticky substance over the wheel. Cigarette ends and other litter stick to the wheel as the motor car drives it over the road. Behind the wheel sits one of the operators who picks the litter off with forks and deposits it behind him in a dustbin. The dustbin is replaced by one of the other three when full.

Above the motor car is a look-out position where the two navigators stand. They look for litter and direct the car towards it. This is done via a system of levers and bells. The upper lever rings the bell on the left of the driver which directs him to the right, and the lower lever rings the bell on the right which directs him to the left.

Write the instructions you would give to someone taking the job of navigator for the first time. Use the key words to help you.

Key words
1 Stand/look-out position
2 See/litter/direct car
3 Turn right/upper lever
4 Turn left/lower lever

Listening

Mark the position of the call box with a cross.
Trace the route to Fiona's friend's house on the map.

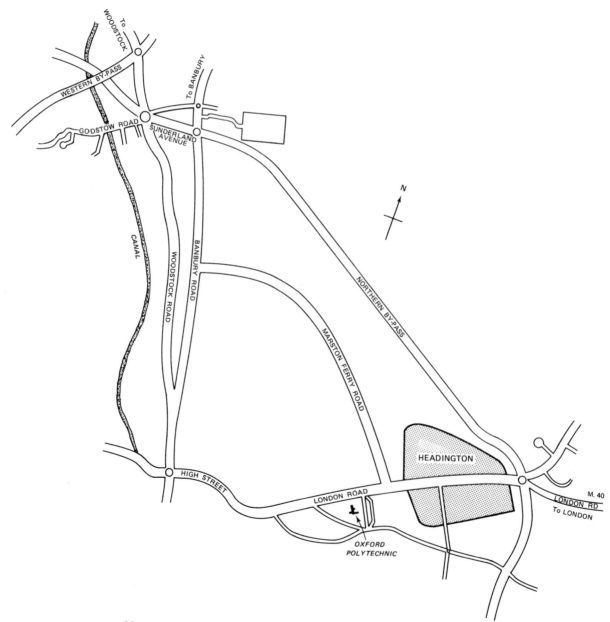

M1 LEICESTER – ALFRETON

Legend

Motorway open with junction numbers	═══③	Service areas open	Ⓢ
A roads	A6	Airport	✈
B roads	B5248		
Unclassified roads	═══		

Mileages

Hull	Inverness	Kendal	Leeds	Leicester	Lincoln	Liverpool	Manchester	Newcastle upon Tyne	Norwich	Nottingham	Oxford
378											
124	294										
55	347	71									
87	436	160	96								
37	406	138	67	51							
128	368	73	73	107	118						
93	367	73	40	87	84	35					
117	262	85	92	181	151	154	129				
143	512	244	173	118	106	215	184	257			
73	411	137	67	25	36	97	70	156	124		
156	505	212	160	69	119	154	142	250	139	94	

Using the information from a motoring handbook, write directions for someone driving from Groby (near Leicester) to Stapleford (near Nottingham).

Listening

Write down the answers to Peter's questions.

> Peter
>
> dont forget to enquire about
> ENGLISH LANGUAGE COURSES - TODAY!
>
> Remember to ask :
> How long ? .....
> Dates? ......
>
> How many hours ? .....
> How many students in class ?.....
> How much ? .....
>
> Deposit ? .....
>
> Accommodation
> How much for:
> Bed and breakfast .....
> Bed and breakfast and dinner.....

Reading and writing

Note the advantages and disadvantages of these five jobs for Mrs Starling.

VACANCIES

Store Detective

for FINGALS Department Store. No previous experience required. 40 hours per week. TUES.– SAT. 9 a.m.– 5.30 p.m. Apply: Mr Jones, Store Personnel Manager, FINGALS, LUTON

Home Help Wanted

6 hours p.w. Mon. Wed. Fri. Hours to suit. £1.50 per hour (no heavy work). Write to: Mrs P. Johnson, 71 North St Luton

Receptionist/Secretary

If you are an experienced secretary with good speeds and a pleasant friendly manner then we have a job for you. TOWERS Hotel is looking for a receptionist to work 8 a.m.–2 p.m. daily. (1 weekend in 3 free) £50 p.w. basic. If you're interested ring us on Luton 73371

Fashion

TREND fashion shop requires part-time assistant to work mornings only. MON.– FRI. 9 a.m.–1 p.m. 3 weeks paid holiday. Apply to: TREND, The High Street, Luton

School meals Supervisor

Waynebridge First School requires a canteen supervisor starting in September. Hours 11 a.m.– 3 p.m. during school terms. Apply to: Education Division, Town Hall, Luton

Job Wanted

Woman, two children of school age, seeks employment. Good typing and shorthand speeds. Clean driving licence. Tel: Luton 534674. Mrs Starling

Job	Advantages	Disadvantages
STORE DETECTIVE		
HOME HELP		
RECEPTIONIST/ SECRETARY		
SHOP ASSISTANT		
SCHOOL MEALS SUPERVISOR		

Using the above say which job is most suitable for Mrs Starling and why.

12 Hiring a car

Listening

Write down the answers to the customer's questions.

CAR HIRE

Self drive - tel: 773141

Leave Friday 7 July and return Monday 10 July.

Things to find out:

Best kind for family of four and camping equip. ?

_____

Pick up after what time ? _____

Return by when ? _____

COST

Basic _____ for how many miles? _____

Per extra mile ? _____

Deposit ? _____

Extra for two drivers ? _____

Prices with/without V.A.T.? _____

Insurance included ? _____

Reading and writing

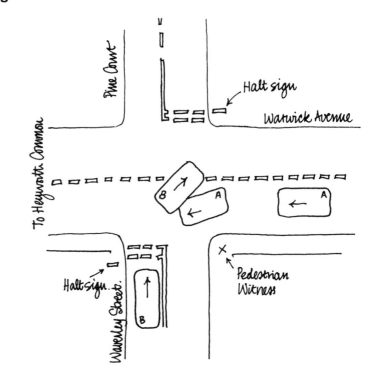

What to do if involved in a road accident
Keep cool and concentrate on the essentials:
 Get help for anyone who is injured.
 Call the police if the accident is serious.
 Collect as much information as possible
for your insurance claim.

Informing the police
Not every accident need be reported to the
police, but there are certain circumstances
where you must stop at the scene of the
accident:
 1 If anyone, apart from yourself, has
been injured.
 2 If any vehicle, apart from your own, has
been damaged.
 3 If certain animals have been injured or
killed.
 4 If there is damage to any property on or
near the road.
 The motorist must give his name, address
and registration number (and the owner's
name and address if he is not the owner) to
anyone who has reasonable grounds for
wanting them.
 When someone has been injured the
motorist must also produce his insurance
certificate.
 Only when names and addresses are not
exchanged after such an accident must the
motorist report it to the police—within 24
hours.

Write a report of the accident as seen from the
position of the pedestrian witness.

Age How it affects the accident rate

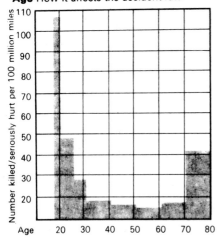

Number killed/seriously hurt per 100 million miles

Age 20 30 40 50 60 70 80

25

Listening

Write the names of the guests at the party above each one.

Reading and writing

Read the letter and decide in which house the party is being held. Tick the correct house and then write to an English friend, inviting him to a party at your home.

```
                    Tudor Cottage,
                     High Street,
                      Bumpton,
                       Oxon,

                    1 July 1980

Dear Jan,
    We are having a party from 7 p.m.
to midnight on Saturday 27 July in
our new house. We do hope you'll come.
    It's very easy to find. When you
come into the village, look for the
main street and we are the third house
on the left as you go towards the
church. It's a black and white house
with an old, white gate, a thatched
roof and a very untidy hedge. You
can park outside.
    Best wishes,
```

Listening

Fill in the times of the appointments. Not all the boxes can be filled in.
Show how the appointments are rearranged to fit in Mr Dennis.

MARCH

26
MON

☐ a.m. Short-list interviews:
☐ Miss Harrison, Miss Jones
☐ Miss Peters

☐ Japanese Agent re contract
↓

? Lunch - Japanese Agent ?

☐ p.m. Lawyer re planning permission

☐ Tutorial - Maria Rosa

☐ Stuart

27
TUES

☐ am. Committee Meeting
☐
↓
Lunch publisher

☐ p.m. Review Report and chief
examiner

☐ Meet Johan Blun's parents

☐ Principal's meeting
↓

28
WED

Reading and writing

Underline the essential details in each message.
Fill in the appointments in the diary.

MON
23 _____
_____
_____

TUES
24 _____
_____
_____

WED
25 _____
_____
_____

THURS
26 _____
_____
_____

FRI
27 _____
_____
_____

SAT
28 _____
_____
_____

SUN
29 _____
_____
_____

Counter No._____   Serial No._____

Office Stamp

POST OFFICE

INLAND TELEGRAM
FOR POSTAGE STAMPS

Charge		Chargeable Words	Sent at/by
Tariff £ excl RP			
VAT £			
RP £		Circulation	

Prefix	Handed in	Service Instructions	Actual Words	TOTAL £

If you wish to pay for a reply insert RP here

To

BLOCK LETTERS THROUGHOUT PLEASE

ARRIVING HURN AIRPORT 10 A.M.
THURSDAY STOP PLEASE MEET ME STOP
LOVE PETER STOP

The particulars on the back of this form should be completed.

Mon. morning
Dropped by but
you are out!
Come over for a
coffee & chat
tomorrow — 11 a.m.
love Jane

Sarah
Garage phoned
— car will be
ready Wed. —
probably.
— phone Wed.
a.m. to check.
John

DAWSON'S DENTAL SURGERY

Reminder

Your next appointment is

24 May 4.30 p.m.

Mr and Mrs Smythe
request the company of

Mr and Mrs Mead

on the occasion of their
25th Wedding Anniversary
on Saturday 28 May at 8 p.m.

R.S.V.P. THE MANOR HOUSE, BURFORD ON AVON, HAMPSHIRE

Listening

Fill in the missing information.

Scotland

Newcastle to Edinburgh	$2\frac{1}{2}$ hours
London to Edinburgh	...... hours
Manchester to Glasgow	4 hours
Bristol to Glasgow	7 hours

Newcastle to Edinburgh	$4\frac{1}{2}$ hours
London to Edinburgh	......hours
Manchester to Glasgow	$8\frac{1}{2}$ hours

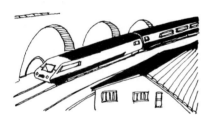

Newcastle to Edinburgh	2 hours
London to Edinburgh	...... hours
Manchester to Glasgow	4 hours
Bristol to Glasgow	$6\frac{1}{2}$ hours

London to Aberdeen	80 mins
London to Edinburgh	.... mins
London to Glasgow	70 mins
London to Inverness	120 mins

Travel to Scotland is not expensive:
From London to Edinburgh by car £......
                  by coach £......
                  by train £......
                  by plane £......

Reading and writing

When in Scotland tourists often forget to follow the *Country Code* below. Read the list of things you should and shouldn't do and write the appropriate number in each picture. Then write a sign underneath each one to stop people from doing things wrong.

THE COUNTRY CODE

1 Guard against fire
2 Fasten all gates
3 Keep dogs under control
4 Keep to paths across farmland
5 Avoid damaging fences, hedges, walls

6 Leave no litter
7 Safeguard water supplies
8 Protect wild life, wild plants and trees
9 Go carefully on country roads

Listening

Make a list of the shops where the items are to be bought.
Label the positions of these shops on the map.

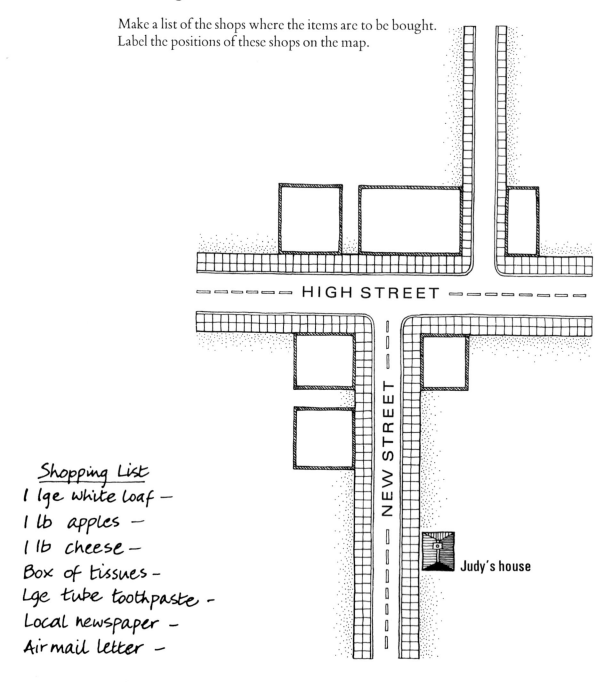

HIGH STREET

NEW STREET

Judy's house

Shopping List
1 lge white loaf –
1 lb apples –
1 lb cheese –
Box of tissues –
Lge tube toothpaste –
Local newspaper –
Air mail letter –

Reading and writing

How much will this shopping cost?

1½ kg flour
1 pkt tea
1 litre oil
2 pkts biscuits
2 cans coke
250g butter
1lb jam
100g coffee

Now make up your own shopping list of
these things and ask a neighbour to work
out how much your shopping will cost.

17 Moving in

Listening

Draw the pieces of furniture in the right places in the room.

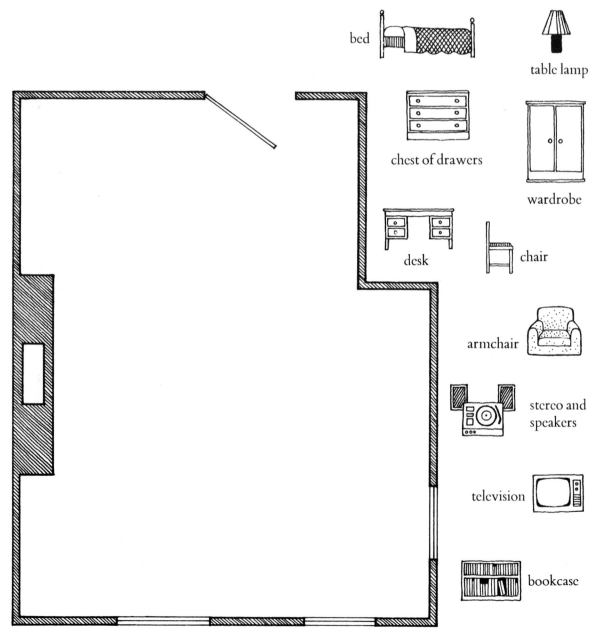

bed

table lamp

chest of drawers

wardrobe

desk

chair

armchair

stereo and speakers

television

bookcase

Reading and writing

Choose three items not mentioned on the tape and order them for Rod Smith's new flat. The address of the flat is 6 Norton Gardens, Brighton. The telephone number is 859067. Make out the order using the name Rod Smith.

1/**Bedside table.** White plastic. 40 × 40 × 40cm. 5846 **£5.65**

2/**Round mirror.** A simple mirror with a coloured plastic frame 24cm diameter. Available in white, yellow, red and brown. 3650 **£1.25**

3/**Duvets.** The best and the cheapest to be found. Machine washable.
Single: 135 × 200cm 8053 **£13.50**
Double: 200 × 200cm 8061 **£15.50**

4/**Pillow.** 45 × 68cm 8088 **£4.00**

5/**Towels.** Thick white cotton towelling with a wide blue stripe.
Hand towel: 55 × 100cm 9122 **£1.10**
Bath towel: 75 × 135cm 9130 **£2.25**

6/**Bed.** The most important single item of furniture you may ever buy. Ours is wood-framed, interior sprung and covered in a choice of really nice blue or brown cotton.
Single: 5853 **£47.00**
Double: 5854 **£63.00**
Large double: 5855 **£89.00**

7/**Rugs.** Handwoven cotton yarn rugs from India. 1378 **£15.95**

8/**Linens.** White sheets, pillowcases and duvet covers.
Single sheet: 1890 **£6.50**
Double sheet: 1871 **£7.50**
Large double sheet: 1892 **£10.50**
Pillowcases: 1900 **£3.45** a pair
Single duvet cover: 3490 **£12.50**
Double duvet cover: 3491 **£15.50**

9/**Blanket.** Thick and cuddly blanket in 100% acrylic fibre which makes it hardwearing and machine washable. Available in blue or brown.

Single: 178 × 230cm 9858 **£5.95**
Double: 230 × 255cm 9866 **£8.25**

10/**Wardrobe.** Plenty of hanging space. 201 × 105 × 56cm 5890 **£75.75**

11/**Dressing table.** The mirror is sold as a separate item.
Dressing table: 67 × 76 × 46cm 5898 **£39.00**
Mirror: 5897 **£17.50**

12/**Three drawer chest.** 67 × 76 × 46cm 5893 **£39.00**

Please complete all details in BLOCK CAPITALS and send this order to: Home Designs Ltd, P.O. Box 20, Western Road, Wellington, Somerset, WW8 1PA. Telephone Wellington (082 347) 76441								

Initials | Surname

Delivery address if different from that shown on left

Address

Initials | Surname

Address

Postcode

Postcode

Telephone nos. work/daytime

Telephone nos. work/daytime

Telephone nos. Home

Telephone nos. Home

Special delivery instructions (e.g. leave in garage):

Office use only	Item description	Item Code No. (if no Code shown item not available by mail)	Colour	2nd choice colour	Qnty.	Item cash price	Total cash price	Office use only
		F						
		F						
		F					£	

35

18 Phoning a garage

Listening

Fill in the information about the car on the grid.

1 gear lever on gearbox
2 exhaust system (and silencer)
3 radiator (cools the water
  which circulates through
  the engine)
4 petrol tank
5 petrol filler
6 headlights

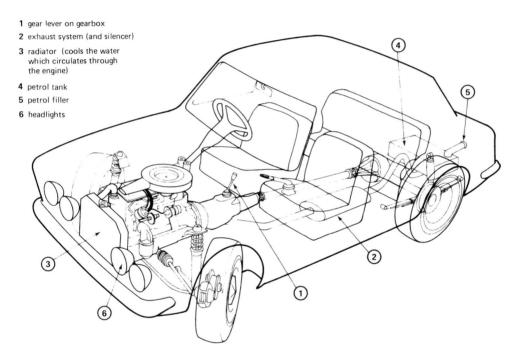

PART OF CAR	O.K.	NEEDS ATTENTION	NOTES
1			
2			
3			
4			
5			
6			

How much will the repairs cost?
– less than £100?
– exactly £100?
– more than £100?

Tick the correct amount.

Reading and writing

Which car would best suit the following people? Give reasons.

1 Mrs Bennett, mother of three (aged 7, 9, 11) needs a car for shopping, taking children to school.

2 Mr Bennett drives 40 miles a day to work. He also needs a car for family holidays etc.

3 Which car would you choose for yourself and why?

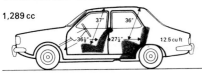

RENAULT 12

1,289 cc

Running costs
Economical – 29 mpg

Verdict
A very likeable medium-sized family saloon. Very comfortable and reliable, with quick acceleration and quiet cruising.

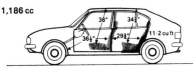

ALFASUD

1,186 cc

Running costs
A little thirsty for 1200 cc – 28 mpg.

Verdict
Great fun to drive, and quite roomy for its size. Fairly reliable, but poor bodywork.

SAAB 99

1,985 cc

Running costs
Latest 2-litre manual versions not tested, earlier 1·85 and 2·0 automatic – 27 mpg.

Verdict
Very solid and well-engineered (particularly for safety). Not a sporty car, but a quiet, comfortable touring saloon. Plenty of luggage space. Overall, quite good value new.

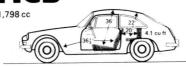

MGB

1,798 cc

Running costs
Petrol: 26 mpg

Verdict
Fast, with good handling and braking. Convertible, one of the few soft top sports cars left.

HONDA CIVIC

1,169 cc

Running costs
Quite economical, 35 mpg

Verdict
Lively small car — fun to drive. Fairly comfortable but road noise makes it less good for long, fast drives. Useful luggage carrier with only two people.

FIAT 126

594 cc

Running costs
Economical 47 mpg, 2-star.

Verdict
Very economical, but not very comfortable, not roomy, and very noisy.

Mrs Bennett

Mr Bennett

My Choice

19   Flat hunting

Listening

List the advantages and disadvantages of the houses, flats etc. advertised. Tick the one chosen.
Answer the questions.

Advantages

FLAT & HOUSE RENTALS

ABINGDON Road, single attic bedsitter and separate small kitchen £38 and £40 deposit, references. Tel. Oxford 774159

ACCOMMODATION Kennington, suit non-smoking person. Tel. Oxford 739676 preferably 6.30 – 7.30 p.m.

AVAILABLE immediately. – Exceptionally attractive well appointed Cotswold House in isolated position 11 miles Oxford, 2 double bedrooms with bathrooms and dressing rooms ensuite, single bedroom, study, drawing room with dining area, large kitchen with laundry off, garden, car-port, stabling etc., long let preferred, £150 pcm. Tel. Witney 2554

AVAILABLE SOON, Furnished Flat, suitable young couple. – Tel. Oxford 40414

BEDSITTING Room available now for lady, Summertown, limited use of kitchen, central heating, h and c water, prefer someone away on Sunday.–Tel. Oxford 55898

BEDSIT £14; Flat £28. Cottage £35.– Tel. Oxford 63785.

ROOM IN shared House, £25 pw, central.– Tel. Oxford 724261

Disadvantages

What kind of accommodation do these people really want?

For how many people?............................

Number of bedrooms?............................

Maximum rent?............................

How far from city centre?..

Anything else?..

Reading and writing

You want to rent a holiday flat in Scotland for one week in August and to sell your electric cooker. Write the two postcards to put in your local shop window.

FREE TO A GOOD HOME!

Long-haired black kittens.
Very friendly, house-trained,
6 weeks old.
Tel: 395 6594

FOR SALE
LADIES' BICYCLE
Good condition, new
tyres, blue + white
£20
Mrs Davies 3 Southgate Rd

TO LET
Cottage in Cornwall. Sleeps 6,
in beautiful village, garden,
sea 2 miles
£ 50 per week
Ring 395 4028 after 6pm.

WANTED

Boat with motor for
family of 4.
No holes please!
Tel 395 3004 at weekends

Listening

In the three blank TVs show which programmes the girl watched. In TV number 1 write
the first programme, in 2 the second and in 3 the third.
Which programmes were on the same channel?

Reading and writing

TV Questionnaire

1. Do you like these types of programmes or not? (Tick or cross)

	You	Student 1	Student 2	Student 3	Total ✓	Total ✗
Films						
News & current affairs						
Discussion						
Sport						
Music						
Comedy						
Serials						
Crime						
Plays						
Documentary						
Other:						

2. What is your favourite programme?
   You:
   Student 1:
   Student 2:
   Student 3:

3. What programme do you like least?
   You:
   Student 1:
   Student 2:
   Student 3:

4. What would you like more of?
   You:
   Student 1:
   Student 2:
   Student 3:

5. What would you like less of?
   You:
   Student 1:
   Student 2:
   Student 3:

Crime:
Starsky and Hutch

Music:
Mozart's 'The Marriage of Figaro'

Comedy:
Laugh with Larry

Play:
Hamlet

Sport:
World Cup Football

Film:
High Noon

Discussion:
Expert Ideas on the Oil Crisis

Documentary:
The Sahara Desert

News and current affairs:
Tonight

Discussion:
For and Against Nuclear Power

Music:
Top of the Pops

Documentary:
Life on Earth

Serial:
Dickens's 'David Copperfield'

Play:
Macbeth

Comedy:
Laurel and Hardy

Crime:
Kojak

Film:
Star Wars

Listening

Fill in the missing information on the advertisements. Then complete the message for Ray.

CINEMA: **THE CONTINENTAL SCREEN 1** # Annie Hall TIME: PRICE:	CINEMA: **Yellow Submarine** TIME: PRICE:
CINEMA: **THE CONTINENTAL SCREEN 2** # STAR WARS TIME: PRICE:	CINEMA: The Deer Hunter TIME: PRICE:

Ray
We're going to see _____
at _____. See you outside
the _____ cinema or in
the pub opposite.
Love from Dick, Diana, Mary

Reading and writing

You want to book two tickets for *Julius Caesar* for a Friday evening in October, but any Saturday in October would also be all right. Fill in the booking form below.

Royal Shakespeare Company
Stratford-upon-Avon

Performance Schedule

Sat 29 Sep 7.30	**J CAESAR**	
Mon 1 Oct 7.30	**J CAESAR**	
Tue 2 Oct 6.30pn	**J CAESAR**	
Wed 3 Oct 7.30	**J CAESAR**	
Thu 4 Oct 7.30	**MERRY WIVES**	
Fri 5 Oct 7.30	**OTHELLO**	
Sat 6 Oct 2.00m	**TWELFTH NGT**	
Sat 6 Oct 7.30	**CYMBELINE**	
Mon 8 Oct 7.30	**CYMBELINE**	
Tue 9 Oct 7.30	**J CAESAR**	
Wed 10 Oct 7.30	**J CAESAR**	
Thu 11 Oct 2.00m	**TWELFTH NGT**	
Thu 11 Oct 7.30	**MERRY WIVES**	
Fri 12 Oct 7.30	**J CAESAR**	
Sat 13 Oct 1.30m	**OTHELLO**	
Sat 13 Oct 7.30	**TWELFTH NGT**	
Mon 15 Oct 7.30	**J CAESAR**	
Tue 16 Oct 7.30	**TWELFTH NGT**	
Wed 17 Oct 7.30	**OTHELLO**	
Thu 18 Oct 2.00m	**J CAESAR**	
Thu 18 Oct 7.30	**J CAESAR**	
Fri 19 Oct 7.30	**CYMBELINE**	
Sat 20 Oct 2.00m	**MERRY WIVES**	
Sat 20 Oct 7.30	**OTHELLO**	
Mon 22 Oct 7.30	**MERRY WIVES**	
Tue 23 Oct 7.30	**J CAESAR**	

Wed 24 Oct 7.30	**TWELFTH NGT**
Thu 25 Oct 2.00m	**TWELFTH NGT**
Thu 25 Oct 7.30	**CYMBELINE**
Fri 26 Oct 7.30	**OTHELLO**
Sat 27 Oct 2.00m	**MERRY WIVES**
Sat 27 Oct 7.30	**J CAESAR**
Mon 29 Oct 7.30	**TWELFTH NGT**
Tue 30 Oct 7.30	**MERRY WIVES**
Wed 31 Oct 7.30	**J CAESAR**
Thu 1 Nov 2.00m	**J CAESAR**
Thu 1 Nov 7.30	**TWELFTH NGT**
Fri 2 Nov 7.30	**OTHELLO**
Sat 3 Nov 2.00m	**MERRY WIVES**
Sat 3 Nov 7.30	**CYMBELINE**

Please note: the performances on 7 August and 2 October start at 6.30 pm, and the matinee performances on 8, 13, 15, 20 September and 13 October start at 1.30 pm. Performance details are published in good faith but changes may occasionally be necessary.
pn = press night
m = matinee
p = preview*
c = concert
*Revisions may be made to a production following its first performance. For this reason this performance is designated a preview.

Julius Caesar

New Production
Cast includes:
Peter Clough — *Octavius*
Ben Kingsley — *Brutus*
James Laurenson — *Cassius*
Nigel Terry — *Casca*
David Threlfall — *Mark Antony*
John Woodvine — *Julius Caesar*
Director — Barry Kyle
Designer — Christopher Morley

Music — James Walker
Lighting — Brian Harris

Shakespeare wrote *Julius Caesar* in 1599 and it was one of the first plays that his company, The Lord Chamberlain's Men, presented at their new Globe Theatre in the same year. It was a favourite until the closing of the theatres in 1642 and was acted several times at Court.

Press reviews will first appear on 3 October.

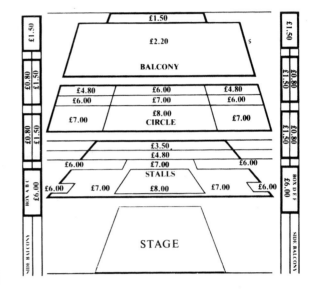

How to use this form: Complete the form in block letters giving alternative dates and prices where possible. If you are paying by cheque please make it payable to the Royal Shakespeare Theatre, *but leave the actual amount open, stating only an upper limit.* Please send completed form (having checked that dates correspond to performances of play you require) with remittance to the Box Office, Royal Shakespeare Theatre, Stratford-upon-Avon, Warwickshire CV37 6BB. *Remember to enclose stamped addressed envelope.*

I apply for the tickets entered below and have given alternative dates and prices.

I enclose s.a.e. and an open cheque limited to the value of £..............

Please note discount for members of the RSC Mailing List has now been discontinued.

Full/Associate Membership No.

Name

Address

Tel. Home   Tel. Business

Date

Date 1st choice	Matinee or Evening	Alternative Dates	Matinee or Evening	Number of Tickets	Price	Alternative Prices	OFFICE USE ONLY

43

Listening

Put number 1 in the box beside the cartoon which illustrates the first conversation.
Make a list of the important words which helped you reach this conclusion.
Do the same for conversations 2, 3 and 4.

Reading and writing

Write down where you would expect to see these.

Directions. Empty contents of a packet of Sainsbury's Blancmange Powder into a 1½ pint basin. From a pint of milk take enough to mix the powder to a smooth paste. Boil the remainder of the milk with 2 tablespoonfuls of sugar. Pour onto the mixture stirring well. Return to saucepan and boil for two minutes stirring all the time. Pour into wetted mould and leave to set.

T E GULLIKSON and I R GUL-LIKSON (US) beat O Bengston (Sweden) and R Fisher (US) 7—5, 7—5, 6—2; R J Carmichael (Australia) and Teacher (US) beat V I Eke (Australia) and W J Farrel (GB) 6—3, 7—6, 6—4, C S Dibley and B D Drewett (Australia) beat B Manson and A J Pattison (US) 6—7, 6—3, 6—2, 3—6, 10—8.

2 DESCRIPTION *SIGNALEMENT*

	Bearer Titulaire	**Spouse** Epouse
Occupation___ Profession		
Place of birth___ Lieu de naissance		
Date of birth___ Date de naissance		
Residence___ Résidence		
Height___ Taille	m	m
Distinguishing marks___ Signes particuliers		

CHILDREN *ENFANTS*

Name Nom	**Date of birth** Date de naissance	**Sex** Sexe

Usual signature of bearer___
Signature du titulaire

Usual signature of spouse___
Signature de son épouse

English Beef
Mince per lb _____ **56p**

Boneless
Roasting (back rib) per lb _____ **£1.02**

English Pork
Boneless Roasting
(shoulder) per lb _____ **79p**

Provisions Counter

Freshly Sliced Danish Prime
Unsmoked Middle Cut Rashers per lb **78p**

Freshly Cut Imported
Cheddar Cheese per lb _____ **69p**

Freshly Cut
Dutch Edam Cheese per lb _____ **59p**

Fill in this identity card for yourself in block letters.

STUDENT IDENTITY CARD

ATTACH PHOTO. HERE	DATE OF BIRTH	Nᵒ A 489491
	NAME	
	FORENAME	
	NATIONALITY	
	SIGNATURE	

EDUCATIONAL ESTABLISHMENT

VALID UNTIL

PLACE AND DATE

Add the chicken meat and still stirring cook for four minutes more. Stir in the ginger, soy sauce, sherry, pepper, salt and 12 fluid ounces (1½ cups) of the chicken stock. Reduce the heat to low and simmer for forty minutes. Stir in the cornflour paste and simmer for two minutes. Add the cream, stir well and cook for one minute more.

23 Following instructions

Listening

Which sport is being taught in the first conversation? Put number 1 in the box beside the photo. Make a list of the important words which helped you reach this conclusion. Do the same for conversations 2 and 3.

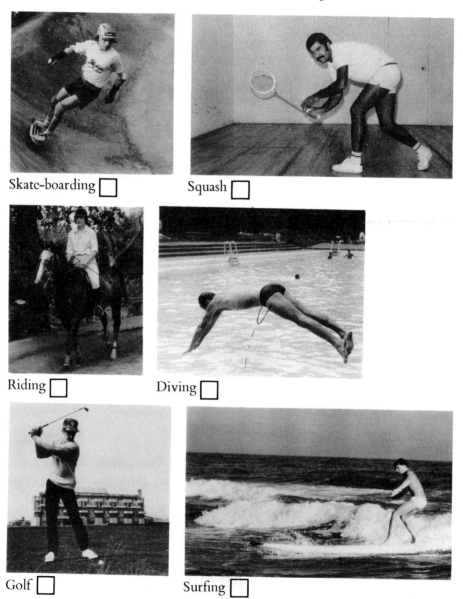

Skate-boarding ☐   Squash ☐

Riding ☐   Diving ☐

Golf ☐   Surfing ☐

46

Reading and writing

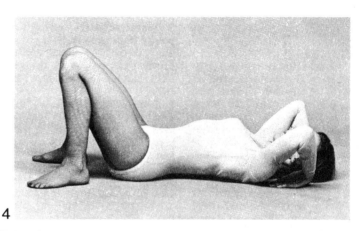

Match three of the above pictures (1, 2, 3 or 4) with the instructions below (A, B, or C). Write the correct numbers in the boxes below and then write instructions to go with the other picture.

A Kneel on the floor. Lean back and hold your legs just above the ankles with each hand. Keep your arms straight. Look up.

B Lie with your knees bent and your feet flat on the floor. Put your hands flat on the floor on either side of your head. Keep your head on the floor and look up.

C Put your hands and feet flat on the floor. Raise your body as high in the air as possible, with your knees bent a little but your arms straight. Look down at the floor.

D

Listening

Tick the cartoon which illustrates the story most accurately.

Reading and writing

What do you think they are saying?
Complete the cartoons in your own words.

Listening

First of all try to guess the place and the object. These are not mentioned on the tape. Then identify the face.

Familiar Place... but where?

Familiar Face...
but whose?

Familiar Object... but what?

They look the same but...

... there are ten differences between these two pictures. Can you spot them?

In the bottom picture put a ring around each difference mentioned. Try to find the missing difference not mentioned on the tape.

Reading and writing

Do these puzzles.

Jim's Christmas List

'What do you want for Christmas?' asked Jim's mother.

'Oh, all sorts of things,' replied Jim. 'I'll make a list of them.'

This he did, but his baby brother found the list and tore it into three strips, then tore the middle strip into eight pieces. His mother put the two large strips together, but they didn't make much sense.

Can *you* work out what Jim wanted for Christmas?

A Party Invitation

Can you read it?

Jim wants for Christmas:

1 ....
2 ....
3 ....
4 ....
5 ....
6 ....
7 ....
8 ....

The invitation says:

Dear ...
We ...

Listening

Tick the photographs of the man and woman described. Make two lists of the words that helped you make your choice, one list for the man and one for the woman.

Man

Woman

Reading and writing

Fill in the questionnaire.
Compare answers with a neighbour.

Somewhere there is Someone who is Right for You.

DON'T GAMBLE ON FINDING YOUR IDEAL PARTNER

Start here

1 BY TICKING THE PHOTO THAT APPEALS MOST TO YOU

2 Do you consider yourself:

Shy: ☐
Extrovert: ☐
Adventurous: ☐
Family type: ☐
Clothes-conscious: ☐

Generous: ☐
Outdoor type: ☐
Creative: ☐
Practical: ☐
Intellectual: ☐

3 Indicate which activities and interests you enjoy by placing a '1' (one) in the appropriate box. If you dislike a particular activity, write a '0' (nought) in the box. If you have no preference, leave the column blank.

Pop music: ☐
Fashion: ☐
Pubs and clubs: ☐
Sport: ☐
Pets: ☐
Folk music: ☐
Jazz: ☐
Travelling: ☐

Cinema: ☐
Good food: ☐
Politics: ☐
Classical music: ☐
Art/Literature: ☐
'Live' theatre: ☐
Science or technology: ☐

Creative writing/painting: ☐
Poetry: ☐
Philosophy/Psychology/Sociology: ☐
History/Archeology: ☐
Conversation: ☐

4 BLOCK CAPITALS ONLY—ONE LETTER PER SPACE —LEAVE BLANKS WHEN REQUIRED

Your Sex ⎽⎽ M or F
Your Age ⎽⎽ yrs
Your Height ⎽⎽ m ⎽⎽ cm

Age I would like to meet ⎽⎽ MIN ⎽⎽ MAX

Christian Name (one only)

Surname

Address

Nationality ⎽⎽⎽⎽⎽⎽⎽ Religion ⎽⎽⎽⎽⎽⎽⎽

Occupation ⎽⎽⎽⎽⎽⎽⎽⎽⎽⎽⎽⎽⎽⎽

5 I enclose 2 first class stamps for postage of my free computer test and brochure. I am genuinely interested in finding my ideal partner.

SIGNED ⎽⎽⎽⎽⎽⎽⎽⎽⎽⎽⎽

Send today to: Dateline, Dept. (OBJ), Singles House, 23/25 Abingdon Rd., London, W.8. (01-937 6503)

LONDON PARIS BONN GENOA

Dateline leaves nothing to chance